JUL 01

Grandmothers at Work

Meet My Grandmother

She's a Deep-Sea Explorer

★ ★ ★

By Lisa Tucker McElroy
(with help from Russell T. Mead)
Photographs by Joel Benjamin
and Mark Gardner

THE MILLBROOK PRESS
BROOKFIELD, CONNECTICUT

This book is for Zoe's nonna, Erminia Forcellati, a remarkable grandmother.

Nonna, without your help, this book never would have been written.

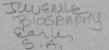

ACKNOWLEDGMENTS

Tamara Miller and Rich Mead; Liz Taylor and Ian Griffith; the DOER staff; Maureen Fulton;
Maryhelen Shuman-Groh; Dan Norman; Lori Watson and Camden Watson Gardner;
Ken Peterson and the staff of the Monterey Bay Aquarium, Monterey, CA;
Dr. Todd Shapiro and his office staff; Dr. Rick Goldstein and his office staff; the McElroy family;
the Tucker family; the D'Esposito and Forcellati families;
my sweet Zoe; and my wonderful husband Steve.

Photographs courtesy of p. 7: Michele Mattei Productions; pp. 5, 8, 16: Jan Sonnenmair/*People Weekly*, copyright © Time, Inc.;
p. 11: The cover of *Hello Fish!* is reproduced with permission of the National Geographic Society. Jacket photograph
by Wolcott Henry. Jacket design copyright © 1999 the National Geographic Society; p. 25: Liz Taylor.
The photos on pages 11, 20-23, 29-30 were taken at the Monterey Bay Aquarium.

Library of Congress Cataloging-in-Publication Data
McElroy, Lisa Tucker.
Meet My grandmother : she's a deep-sea explorer / by Lisa Tucker McElroy (with help from Russell Mead);
photographs by Joel Benjamin and Mark Gardner.
p. cm. – (Grandmothers at work)
Summary: Describes the life of this groundbreaking marine biologist and diver,
as seen through the eyes of her grandson.
ISBN 0-7613-1720-1 (lib. bdg.)
1. Earle, Sylvia A., 1935-—-Juvenile literature. 2. Marine biologists—United States—Juvenile literature.
3. Women marine biologists—United States—Juvenile literature. [1. Earle, Sylvia A., 1935-
2. Marine biologists. 3. Women—Biography.] I. Benjamin, Joel, ill. II. Gardner, Mark, 1960- ill. III. Title.
QI191.3.E2 M31 2000
578.77'092—dc2   [B]   00-023091

Published by The Millbrook Press, Inc.
2 Old New Milford Road, Brookfield, Connecticut 06804
www.millbrookpress.com

I think that getting near a shark

would be scary, but my grandmother does it all the time. She says that if you mind your own business, sharks will mind theirs. It's more dangerous to drive in traffic than it is to swim with sharks! The only time a shark got too close to her, G-mom just thumped him on the nose with her flipper and he swam right off.

My name is Russell Mead and I'm ten years old. My grandmother, Sylvia Earle, is a deep-sea explorer.

Kelp often washes in from the ocean onto the shore. It's brown and a little bit slimy.

G-mom is trained as a marine biologist and an ecologist. She studies plants and animals that live in the sea and tries to figure out how to conserve, or save, these types of oceanic life. G-mom says that marine life is enchanting and beautiful and wonderful. She likes her job a lot.

To study marine life, G-mom often goes down deep in the ocean wearing scuba gear or in a submersible, a machine that she can sit in underwater. In fact, G-mom has walked deeper down on the ocean floor than anyone else has. That's why some people call her "Her Deepness." It's a term of respect, because G-mom works so hard underwater. I think it's really cool that G-mom gets to walk around on the bottom of the ocean. Not many kids can say that their grandmothers hang out with barracudas and sea horses!

Actually, G-mom doesn't really have

a regular job. She works in all kinds of places: her office in Oakland, California; the National Geographic offices in Washington, D.C. (she's the magazine's "Explorer-in-Residence"); on research ships; underwater; and in aquariums and schools across the country. When she's not in or on the water, she is looking through a microscope, studying books, learning about geology and chemistry and physics, and talking to audiences. G-mom talks to *everyone* about the oceans: corporate executives, other scientists, governmental officials, and especially us, her grandchildren. We hear *a lot* about what's going on in the ocean!

★

I think the Styrofoam moray eel on top of G-mom's computer is really cool. My brother, Kevin, likes her angelfish screensaver.

★

Taylor and Morgan
can sit in the subs with
G-mom on the shore, but
only adults can sit in
them underwater.

Our whole family is really involved in DOER, G-mom's business in Oakland. It's called that because its old name, Deep Ocean Exploration and Research, was too long. DOER helps to build the submersibles that G-mom and other scientists use for their research. The subs – that's what we call them – are like big space suits with room to move around, and some of them have computer-controlled arms and stuff. My cousin Morgan started going into the DOER office with Aunt Elizabeth when he was only a few days old, and my cousins Taylor and Morgan like to sit in the submersibles with G-mom.

Unfortunately, I'm too big to get inside the submersibles with G-mom now; I'd have to be two or three years old to fit. I want to learn to use one by myself when I'm a little older.

G-mom also writes books about the oceans and her experiences in them. Some of them are for adults; they talk about her work as a scientist and her hopes for our planet. Some of them are for kids and are about the kinds of plants and animals that live in the ocean. My cousin Taylor thought it was neat when we saw one of G-mom's children's books in a store.

The fish on the cover of *Hello, Fish!* is a clownfish. Taylor liked it so much that G-mom bought him a big plush one for a toy.

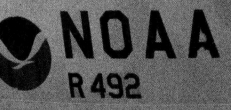

NOAA stands for National
Oceanographic Atmospheric
Administration.

of G-mom's work is her long research trips. Every year, she goes out on research ships for four whole months. The trips are usually in the summer, when it's warm. The ships go to marine sanctuaries—places where marine life is protected—around the United States. Last year G-mom went to nine sanctuaries on her research trips. This year she'll go to at least four.

When G-mom and the scientists she works with go out on the research ships, they look at what marine life in the ocean is like right now. They want to describe it and write about it so that future scientists who study marine life can make comparisons. For example, scientists in the year 2100 might want to study the types of starfish or algae in the Gulf of Mexico. Then they might want to compare their research to G-mom's to see whether starfish and algae are thriving—doing well—or having trouble surviving.

On the research ships, G-mom works

with lots of other scientists. They send submersibles and scuba divers down into the ocean to take pictures and collect samples of organisms that live there. They are always happy when they find many species in a small cove, because the more species they see in a single area, the healthier the water and habitat are.

★

When the scientists want to lower the sub into the water, a snorkeler goes down first to make sure that everything is working OK.

G-mom doesn't design the submersibles herself. She tells engineers what she needs a machine to do, and then they build it. Sometimes, when she has an idea for a submersible, they can build it pretty quickly. It can take many years to get the money to build submersibles, though. Right now G-mom has ideas for some submersible designs, but she is still looking for the money to build them. Fund-raising is a huge part of her work. The submersibles are very expensive!

★

When the crane lowers this sub onto the ocean floor, the scientist inside can see fish swimming all around him.

Sometimes, if it rains really hard, I look out my window and wonder whether G-mom is OK out there on the ocean. I know she is, though. G-mom has been in lots of big storms at sea. She says that they can be really beautiful. There's not much you can do when a storm comes up except to hang on tight! G-mom has even been underwater when a huge storm came up. She couldn't come up to the surface quickly because her body had to adjust to the change in pressure, so she just stayed put! Even though the fish were swimming pretty hard and the water was rough, everything turned out OK.

I enjoy going on short day trips with G-mom, but sometimes I feel a little queasy when I'm on a boat. I asked G-mom if *she* ever feels seasick on the ships. She said that she is usually too busy to get seasick! Besides, once she's been at sea for a while, she gets her sea legs. Each time she goes out, though, she can get sick again until she gets used to the motion of the water. She says that most people do OK with medicine for seasickness. Of course, she points out that those medicines weren't available to Christopher Columbus and his crew.

★

Even when she's at sea, G-mom stays in touch with us by phone. Her cell phone works up to a few miles offshore, and she even has a special phone that she can use when her cellular phone won't work.

17

G-mom was one of the first women

to enter her field of science. Now there are lots of women who explore and study the oceans, but that wasn't always true. As recently as forty years ago, women were considered to be bad luck at sea.

G-mom has to be in great shape because swimming in the water takes a lot of energy. It can be hard for her to find time to work out because she travels so much, but she says that it's OK because she gets a lot of exercise running through airports!

★

G-mom uses this digital video camera to film the launch and recovery of her subs. When the workers are lowering the subs by crane, she has to wear a hard hat to protect herself in case of an accident.

In this photo, G-mom is showing another scientist how the manipulator hand works on the sub. The hand pinches things so that it can pick them up.

around the world a lot when she's exploring the oceans, she also spends a lot of time at home in California with my brother and cousins and me. She loves to teach us things about the ocean and the different fish, animals, and plants that live there. One of our favorite places to go is the Monterey Bay Aquarium on the coast of the Pacific Ocean in Monterey.

★

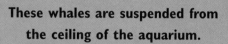

These whales are suspended from the ceiling of the aquarium.

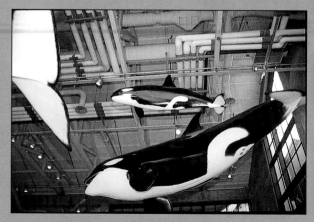

visit the aquarium. She thinks that aquariums are important, because when people visit them, they learn to love marine life and want to help save it. Lots of the exhibits at the aquarium help people learn about the dangers our oceans face. Our family really loves to go there because there are lots of fish and sea animals from around the world. Where else can you see sea otters and sharks and sea anemones without even getting your feet wet?

★

These anchovies can swim incredibly fast. They use a scissors kick to travel in schools, or groups, of three thousand or more.

aquariums are halfway houses, or safe places away from home.

At the aquarium, there's one exhibit where kids can look at sea creatures up close and smell them and touch them. My cousin, Taylor, and my brother, Kevin, especially like that one. G-mom even joins in. She's not afraid to touch slimy things like a lot of adults are.

At this exhibit, Kevin, Taylor, and I are touching lots of kinds of plants and animals: starfish, hermit crabs, sea cucumbers, seaweed, and more!

G-mom likes to take us to some of the ecology exhibits, but one of *our* favorite places at the aquarium is the giant jellyfish tank. Jellyfish glow in the dark! They have lots of tentacles and are incredibly beautiful.

The giant jellyfish are called
sea nettles, but G-mom says
they won't sting unless you
bother them.

23

G-mom loves to cook, and we love her food.She makes great steamed artichokes and terrific rigatoni, not to mention her brownies and cupcakes. Yum! She also really likes gardening. She plants berries and other fruits in the garden so that butterflies and birds will visit. Of course, she enjoys playing with the little kids and riding bikes with Kevin and me.

G-mom and Taylor think this toy squid is pretty funny. It's bigger than Taylor is!

The long brown stuff is egregea, or feather boa kelp. G-mom likes to wear it around her neck!

All of us kids love to go to the beach with G-mom. We put on shorts and sandals and windbreakers when we go. We like to get our feet wet and feel the sand between our toes. Even though it can get windy and chilly out there, G-mom loves to show us the seaweed that washes up on shore and help us listen to the sounds of the ocean in conch shells.

She also loves it when we take her by the hand, lead her into the waves or up onto the rocks, and show her what interests *us*.

★

All of the rocks on this beach were once underwater. When we climb up, we can see far out into the ocean. Boats look like tiny dots!

27

When G-mom was my age, she would use a face mask and look down into the shallow water near her house. She says that that face mask was like a magic window: She could see everything below but breathe freely in the water. That experience led her to a career as a deep-sea explorer.

I think about that when I take my face mask and look at the beautiful, enchanting, mysterious world beneath the surface of the ocean. It's kind of like looking into G-mom's office—well, at least the waiting room. Someday, I'd like to go right down to the bottom of the ocean with her and help her save the plants and animals.

The sea is as near as we come to another world
Anne Stevenson

Maybe I'll even get to swim
with the sharks, just like **she** does.

If You Want to Be a Deep-Sea Explorer . . .

Learn as much about as many things as you can. Of course, your science and math studies are particularly important.

Read lots of books about our planet and the oceans. As a deep-sea explorer, you will want to know a great deal about the sea and the many plants and creatures that live there.

Watch documentaries on television. Public television sponsors many excellent programs about ocean exploration.

Visit the ocean. If you live near the coast, walk along the beach in the different seasons and look at what you find there. If you do not live near the ocean, encourage your parents to take you there for a vacation.

Learn to swim and snorkel. With a face mask, you can see the wonderful world below the ocean's surface.

Question everything and never stop. Scientists are constantly asking, "Why?" You will want to ask, "Why are there high and low tides?" "Why can fish breathe underwater when I can't?" "Why is the ocean so deep?" and many other questions.

Help protect the environment. By recycling, preserving, and respecting the Earth's resources, you will help keep the waters clean and safe for living creatures.

Observe life in your own backyard. Crawl with the caterpillars, climb a tree to see a bird's nest, dig in the soil to watch the earthworms. By studying plants and animals on land, you will learn about scientific discovery, and you will make better observations at sea.

Get wet!